Fishing Southern Kentucky and Northern Tennessee Waters

Fishing Southern Kentucky and Northern Tennessee Waters

BY

LOY R. MILAM

P.O. Box 81
Tompkinsville, KY 42167
2014

Fishing Southern Kentucky and Northern Tennessee Waters

© Pioneer Paths Publishing, 2014. All rights reserved. No part of this book may be reproduced, except in printed form as a matter of reference. Printed in the United States.

ISBN 978-0-9906363-0-4

Fishing Southern Kentucky and Northern Tennessee Waters

Introduction

I worked for several years as an outdoor editor in southern Kentucky and have also contributed a number of outdoor articles and photographs to many outdoor magazines throughout my career as a journalist. I have been blessed to live in one of the best fishing locations in the country. Southern Kentucky and northern Tennessee has a number of trophy fisheries, including Dale Hollow Lake which straddles the Kentucky-Tennessee state line and is home of the world record smallmouth bass; the Cumberland River which is a trophy trout fishery maintained by the *Kentucky Department of Fish & Wildlife* and has also produced numbers of trophy walleye, sauger, and monster stripers over the years; Barren River Lake, which has an excellent population of bass and crappie; Cordell Hull, which produces a number of different species, including largemouth bass, walleye, sauger, and stripers; and Lake Cumberland, which is another excellent smallmouth and striper lake.

In my career as a journalist I have been fortunate to fish all of these waters with very knowledgeable anglers and have shared their knowledge through my newspaper, magazine, and online articles. I have written literally hundreds of articles on fishing southern Kentucky and northern Tennessee and have also served as a fishing guide on many of these same waters. In this book I share with you what I have learned over the years from these expert anglers.

Fishing Southern Kentucky and Northern Tennessee Waters

Obviously this information will aid the reader if he or she has the opportunity to make a fishing trip to southern Kentucky or northern Tennessee, but it will also make you a better fisherman on your own home waters. Many of the techniques I discuss in this book will easily translate into success on your own favorite fishing spot.

Best of luck,

Loy R. Milam, 2014

Loy Milam with his grandson, Austin Graves, with a big Cumberland River striper *"Rock fish"*

Understanding Water Clarity

Jared Adams of Mount Juliet, Tennessee with a nice smallmouth bass taken on a jig at Dale Hollow Lake.

Anglers realize the effects of water temperature on fish, but there is also another component of water that needs to be considered; water color. Water color – or more properly water clarity – affects the environment and habits of fish, and in turn, the methods and means the successful angler must use to catch them. No lake is perfectly clear. All are colored to some degree; some more than others.

Fishing Southern Kentucky and Northern Tennessee Waters

Lakes gain their color from a number of sources. Differences in water clarity are primarily caused by the presence (or lack) of dissolved substances and/or suspended particles in the water. Particles include free-floating algae, called phytoplankton, as well as other solids including sand, clay, or debris from the surrounding land that has either been washed in or brought in by wind or rain. These particles absorb and scatter sunlight as light passes through the water, therefore water clarity decreases as the amount of these particles increase.

Generally speaking, lakes fall under one of three conditions: *clear*, *stained* and *dark*. But how clear is clear? How stained is stained? How dark is dark? These are obviously all relative questions. What one angler sees as stained could be perceived as dark by another. If we are to make accurate determinations of water clarity, we must have some standard with which to work.

Biologists today often use a device to gauge water clarity that originated on the Mediterranean Sea in 1865. It is called the *Secchi Disc* which was invented by Pietro Angelo Secchi, a scientific advisor in Rome in the mid-1800s, and used to measure the water clarity of the Mediterranean. The *Secchi Disc* is an 8-inch disc that is either solid white or alternating black and white quadrants. The disc is tied to a string with measurement markings and is lowered into the water, and the measurement is taken when the disc vanishes from the observer's sight, thus measuring clarity.

Anglers who want a close estimate of water clarity based on the *Secchi Disc* concept can use a clean white lure such as a jig or spinnerbait. If the submerged lure can still be seen at a depth of 6 feet or more on a sunny day, the water is considered *clear*. If the lure vanishes between 2 to 6 feet, the water is *stained*. If you are unable to see the lure at depths less than 2 feet, the water is *dark*. Now that we've determined how to gauge clarity, how can we use this information to fine-tune our approach?

First, we must understand how clarity, or the lack of it, affects the feeding habits of bass. Bass have two primary methods of searching for food: sight and sound. Even though the ability of fish to pick up sound vibrations is keen, when possible, most predator fish will rely more on sight. In relatively clear water that's possible. But when the water turns to heavily stained or dark, then sound becomes the dominant means of searching out forage.

Feeding times can also be affected by water clarity. For the same reasons mentioned above, fish living in dark waters will feed more during the brighter hours of daylight when visibility is best. Conversely, clear water fish tend to feed more at low light hours. Because of limited light penetration, fish in dark or heavily stained waters tend to be shallow, while fish in clear water are more often found deep.

Once the clarity situation is established for a specific lake or pond, lure selection and presentation becomes a simple process. Common sense tells us that noisy, bright-colored lures will be more effective in dark water. Choosing the lighter colors will make detection easier, while vibrating lures like spinnerbaits, buzzbaits and rattle-type baits will make the offering easier to locate. Using the same techniques in clear water, though, can have a negative effect. Fish in clear water tend to be spooked by noisy presentations. For those situations anglers should tone their offerings down with less vibration and flash.

A few other differences that are worth remembering are that fish in clearer water will roam more, chase lures more readily, be more likely to school and prefer smaller lures presented with accurate life-like action. You can get by with sloppier presentations while fishing in dark water, but should expect to find fish more scattered, more object-oriented, but less spooky.

Fishing success is a balancing act where the angler must make critical decisions based on a number of variables. Water clarity plays an important role in those decisions. Approach it with a little thought and you're well on your way to clearing up the subject of clarity.

Art Laker with a nice Dale Hollow smallmouth bass.

Bass Fishing and Sound

If you have ever been bass fishing at night, the question of how bass locate an artificial lure has probably crossed your mind more than once. Not only can a bass detect noisy baits like spinners and gurgling surface baits, but they can also pick up such baits as a solid black plastic worm on nights void of moonlight with apparent ease. How? Vision is extremely poor at best and vibration doesn't even come close to the churning produced by the blades of a spinnerbait or the slurping of a topwater bait. The only sound produced by the plastic worm is just the faint vibration of the fluttering tail and the tick or thump of the sinker striking rocks, wood or the bottom, and yet, detection nears perfection. How? Good question.

Biological research has shown that fish detect sound in two ways: 1) by hearing through an inner ear, and 2) by feeling through their lateral line. While both systems will overlap at certain frequencies, as a general rule, sounds above 100 cycles per second (Hz) are heard through the inner ear apparatus and sounds below 100 Hz are felt through the lateral line. Both systems are reportedly equipped with sensory cells oriented in opposite directions to help fish pinpoint the source of the sound. In addition, the internal swim bladder – a gas-filled sac used for floatation – assists the inner ear with sound interpretation. The swim bladder membrane compresses when exposed to sound waves. These compressions are also transmitted to the inner ear, magnifying the interpretation of the sound. Through use of the inner ear, bass can generally detect the direction of sound production at a distance of up to 30 feet.

But how does this information help anglers?

Bass prefer to use their sense of sight to pinpoint prey. However, during low visibility periods (at night or in muddy water) feeding is almost entirely dependent on sound interpretation via the inner ear at a distance and the lateral line to isolate prey and strike. In periods of low visibility anglers can increase their success by using baits that emit a lot of sound such as spinnerbaits and lures with rattles. Since bass are at the top of the food chain as adults, they have little to fear and often strike out of curiosity or sheer aggressiveness towards an unfamiliar trespasser. The opposite is true in clear water where visibility is very good. In high visibility conditions anglers can increase success by toning down their sound presentations by using soft, subtle baits (i.e., weightless flukes and wacky worms) that closely mimic sounds of natural prey.

While research has only scratched the surface on the subject of fish and sound, studies have gone far enough to determine that different frequencies evoke different reactions from fish. Consequently, different lures produce different frequencies. Just as anglers change colors to increase productivity, changing frequencies can also be the ticket to more fish in the livewell. Even a change in retrieve speed can create a change of pitch, causing fish to react more favorably.

As fish continue to grow more educated because of increased fishing pressure, anglers must constantly search for new tricks to fool them into striking lifeless presentations. While sound is not the only answer, it is another stimulus fishermen can use to fine tune their technique. In fact, when you begin looking at baits and grouping them according to sound, it opens up a completely new chapter in modern bass fishing; one that could give you the edge on both the fish and your fishing buddies.

The inner ear of bass has three separate sensory patches that are lined with 20,000 or more hair-like cells that work together to enable bass to distinguish sound frequencies. Andrew Starnes used "sound" techniques to catch this Dale Hollow smallmouth.

Locating Fish According to Temperature and Oxygen Content

In this article we will attempt to answer the most-asked question among anglers: *"Where are the fish?"* A tall order you say? True, if we attempt to do so with maps or directions to the hottest spots on lakes within a 100-mile radius of your specific location. But that's not the way we'll be dealing with the question. Our approach is better. It deals with principals and will better enable you to effectively locate fish anywhere you fish.

To begin with, you need to understand that on any given lake or pond, 90 percent of the catchable fish will likely be concentrated in only 10 percent of the available water... maybe less. To complicate matters, that 10 percent area will change from season to season.

The first thing we must understand is that fish are cold-blooded creatures; their body temperature being regulated by the temperature of their environment. Since fish have virtually no control over their body temperature, in order to function, they must seek out areas of favorable temperatures. We'll call them *"comfort zones."*

But now we are faced with another problem. Not only will temperature affect the location of fish, but available oxygen will as well. Of the two, oxygen is far more important and will even force fish into lower or higher temperatures than those preferred.

Considering both factors through a 12-month period, temperature is the ruling factor during the colder months of the year, while oxygen content is most important when trying to determine locations during the hotter summer months. In the summer, the sun heats the upper depths of the lake, creating a narrow band of water below the surface called the *"thermocline."* Above the thermocline the water is warmer, but also has the best oxygen content. Below the thermocline, the temperature drops sharply, but so does available dissolved oxygen. In most situations, that makes the thermocline area itself the most comfortable zone for fish. Find the thermocline and you'll find fish, especially if it is located at the same level as a channel break or other structure the fish can relate to. Modern sonar units will display thermoclines. If you don't have one, fish breaks and structure in the 12 to 16 foot range on average, deeper if you are fishing a very clear lake. One exception to this rule is those shallow shoreline areas that are shaded and have heavy vegetation. These areas will have high dissolved oxygen content and may be several degrees cooler that adjacent open water.

Fishing Southern Kentucky and Northern Tennessee Waters

It's a different story when fishing the colder months of the year. As the surface water cools in late fall, it becomes more dense and sinks, causing the warmer (less dense) water at the bottom of the lake to rise, resulting in what is called the *"turnover"* where the water in the lake actually turns over. In the process, the entire lake takes on good oxygen content and that's when temperature becomes the ruling factor. Since there is available dissolved oxygen throughout the water table, fish will seek out the most favorable temperature according to depth.

Finding active fish isn't always an easy process. And at some times of the year, it's even harder than others. But the process becomes a lot simpler when you understand that temperature and oxygen play critical roles in where fish will be... and where they won't be.

Derrick Bartley of Tompkinsville, Kentucky with a nice Dale Hollow smallmouth caught by keying in on water temperature and oxygen content.

Fishing Southern Kentucky and Northern Tennessee Waters

Targeting Crappie

My father was never what you would call a bass fisherman, but spent most of his time in search of catfish, and his favorite fish; crappie. In fact, the earliest fishing memories I have were spent in the 1950s and 60s with my father crappie fishing from an enclosed, lighted *"crappie house"* on Buffalo Lake near out hometown of Lubbock, Texas, or trips we took to Possum Kingdom Lake, an impoundment on the Brazos River in Palo Pinto and Young counties, 75 miles west of Fort Worth, Texas. We not only hooked thousands of fish through the years, it also hooked me on fishing. My dad was smart that way; he knew that introducing a youngster to an active and exciting fish – crappie – would open the door for a lasting relationship with the sport.

Crappie are relatively easy to catch and can be found throughout the country. There are two basic sub-species of crappie: the *black crappie* and the *white crappie*. As the names suggest, the black crappie is darker in color than the white, but there are also subtle differences between the two species. As a general rule, black crappie inhabit deeper, clearer bodies of water, while white crappie are more prominent in swallower, stained water. However, very often both species can be found on the same body of water. Black crappie are normally white or gray with dark gray or black spots covering most of its sides. They have 7-8 dorsal spines on the top of its back. The white crappie tends to be lighter in color and often has distinct vertical bars of gray extending down its sides. It has 5-6 dorsal spines. Both have nearly the same feeding patterns and spawning time.

Both black and white crappie are schooling fish and spend a great deal of their time suspended in open water. The spring spawn is an exception to this rule. Once the water temperature reaches 48-51 degrees, crappie begin to migrate toward shallower water in cuts, coves, or along the shoreline in what is known as the *pre-spawn* period. Both species will spawn in shallow water when the water temperature reaches between 52-60 degrees. During both the pre-spawn and spawn periods, crappie can readily be found in and around wood cover that is adjacent to good spawning areas. Most anglers consider crappie to be cover-oriented fish. That's actually misleading because both species of crappie spend most of their time suspended in confined open water. That's not to say that crappie don't relate to cover. They do. Spring and fall are both times of the year when wood cover is the first place anglers should go in search of crappie.

Experienced crappie anglers realize that water temperature is the key to finding crappie. When the surface temperature approaches 60 degrees, both male and female crappie will migrate from deep water and begin staging near shallow spawning areas (key staging areas are drops with plenty of cover that are adjacent to shallow water). As the temperature climbs to 65 degrees, males will move up into shallow cover to begin sweeping out nests.

While spawning activity may occur between 65 to 75 degrees, peak spawning should be expected at 70 degrees, with females moving into the male's selected areas to deposit their eggs.

Immediately following spawning, females return to deeper cover, while males will remain to guard the nests. Eggs normally hatch in about 2 days and males will remain to guard the fry until they leave the nests (2 to 6 days after hatching.)

Sydney Starnes of Tompkinsville, Kentucky with a couple of nice crappie taken from a 100-acre lake which provides the City of Tompkinsville with its water.

Aside from the changes in crappie location prompted by water temperature, crappie by nature are nomads. One tracking study in Tennessee revealed that crappie were recovered as far as 18 miles from the location they were initially tagged. If you find crappie in one location today, there is no guarantee they will be in the same location tomorrow. However, there are some general rules that will help anglers begin their search according to the seasons.

Prior to spawning, crappie usually congregate around the entrance to creek arms, and as the water continues to warm, they will move into the back half of coves to spawn on shallow points, shoreline flats, and around wood structure in 3-5 feet of water. Most crappie will move back to the main lake and suspend near deep channels in the summer, but will migrate back to the creek arms in the fall. As the water cools in winter, crappie again migrate back to the main lake to once again suspend near deep channels.

Fishing for crappie that are holding to structure is a relatively simple matter; just tie on a minnow or jig and work your bait or lure in and around the cover. Running your bait under a bobber will ensure that it remains at a constant depth and results in fewer hang-ups. Just keep in mind that crappie are more prone to move *UP* to take bait rather than *DOWN*. Experiment with different depths to see what produces the best. Targeting suspended crappie will require a little more searching. Using your electronics is a good way to locate suspended crappie. Anglers can also use the *"spider"* method to locate fish in open water.

Jackie Hammer of Glasgow, Kentucky with a nice spring crappie taken at Barren River Lake in south-central Kentucky.

This method involves drifting potential locations with a number of rods in the water at different depths; thus your presentations resemble the legs of a spider. If one depth gets more action than others, change all rods to that depth. A longer, light-action rod with spinning reel is the best setup for this technique. Fishing supply stores carry a variety of excellent crappie rods from 8 to 12 feet, including *Mr. Crappie*, *B&M*,

and *Bass Pro's Crappie Max*. I would also recommend the *Driftmaster* rod holders for *"spider"* fishing, and also either the *Bass Pro* or *Berkley* marker buoys for marking the location of a school of crappie when you find them.

Line sizes vary for crappie presentations. One can use heavier line when fishing in treetops because the limbs break up the outline of the line. When fishing in open water for suspended crappie, 4 to 6 pound test is best. Being able to detect the subtle hit of crappie is also important. For this reason, lines with high visibility are recommended; such as *Mr. Crappie's* Hi-Viz, *Stren's* HiVis Gold, and *Vicious'* HI VIS Yellow.

Top crappie lures for Barren River Lake crappie include the *Bobby Garland Baby Shad, Southern Pro*, and *Panfish Assassin*. Suggested lure weights would include from 1/32 to 1/16 ounce, and 1/8 ounce for deeper presentations.

The daily limit of crappie on Barren River Lake is 30 and the possession limit is 60. Keeper crappie on Barren must be at least 9 inches in length.

The author with a nice crappie caught on a *float-and-fly* jig.

Float-and Fly for Smallmouth Bass

It's funny how terminology plays such an important role in preconceived notions we develop. The initial reaction of most bass fishermen when *Float-and-Fly* is mentioned is to immediately dismiss it by saying something like, "I don't fly fish." Perhaps it is this common misconception that has kept the general population of bass anglers in the dark concerning this big smallmouth bass technique. Trust me... this ain't your grandfather's fly fishing.

Lucas Geralds of Monroe County, Kentucky displays a nice winter smallmouth from Dale Hollow Lake.

Fishing Southern Kentucky and Northern Tennessee Waters

The truth is that the *Float-and-Fly* isn't *fly* fishing at all, but a technique that produces some of Dale Hollow Lake's biggest bronzebacks of the year each winter, beginning around Thanksgiving and running through March.

Before we get into the particulars of the technique, let's look at the daunting objective that the *Float-and-Fly* attempts to accomplish. Since it is a winter technique, it targets bass in their most lethargic state. With water temperatures sometimes in the 40s, smallmouth bass are suspended, their metabolism is the lowest it will be all year, and they will not chase anything. Bass anglers know these are the hardest fish to catch. If you entice them into biting, your presentation has to be S-L-O-W and your lure must be very convincing. But even a cold, lethargic, suspended smallmouth with a low metabolic rate will bite if you dangle a life-like presentation in front of it long enough. The *Float-and-Fly* does exactly that; it presents a *fly* at the level the fish is suspended that simply sits and *"breathes"* until the bass gives in. Now let's talk tackle and technique.

First, we need to get the *fly* out of the ointment. The lure component of this technique is not a Pheasant Tail Nymph or a Light Cahill. In fact, it's not a fly at all... it's a jig. So why call it a *fly*? Perhaps the answer to that question lies in the popularity of the "bread and butter" lure produced by the late Elmer Thompson who founded the *Thompson Fishing Tackle Company* in Knoxville, Tennessee in 1952. Thompson's *Doll*

Fly was a leadhead jig dressed with polar bear hair. At the height of production, Thompson's company produced as many as 75,000 jigs per day and a staggering 27.5 million per year. The term *doll fly* became synonymous with any hair-dressed jig. The deadly hair jig gained popularity with crappie fishermen around the country, but it also caught on with some savvy Tennessee smallmouth anglers; the legendary Billy Westmoreland caught his largest bronesback (10 lbs. 2 oz.) on a yellow *doll fly* tipped with a pork rind at Dale Hollow Lake.

The history of the *Float-and-Fly* technique for smallmouth bass is also of Tennessee origin. Jim Dicken gives credit for the original concept of the technique to an East Tennessee tackle store owner named Charlie Nuckols. According to Dicken, Nuckols came up with the idea when East Tennessee crappie fishermen came into his shop complaining about smallmouth breaking off their *doll flies* while fishing for crappie. Nuckols began experimenting with various ways to use hair jigs to tempt suspended winter smallmouth. The result was the *Float-and-Fly* technique which has evolved over the past few years, aided by Tennessee angler and guide, Bob Coan, and Stephen Headrick of *Punisher Lures*. "I guess the biggest contribution I have made to the technique is pouring the jigs on a #2 hook to get a little more bite in the rig," says Headrick. "Charlie [Nuckols] used the aspirin head jig with a smaller hook which is normally used by crappie fishermen, so I beefed things up to handle smallmouth by going to the #2 hook."

Fishing Southern Kentucky and Northern Tennessee Waters

While individual techniques may vary among anglers, the basic setup for the *Float-and-Fly* technique involves a sturdy drop line (*Fire Line* 8-10 pound test) from a spinning reel and 8-11foot flexible rod, connected to a three-way swivel, a leader line of 6-pound fluorocarbon tied to one of the remaining eyes of the swivel at a length equivalent to the depth of the bait fish and suspended bass (8-18 feet), a customized Styrofoam bobber clipped to the remaining eye of the swivel, and a 1/16 or 1/32 ounce hair/feather jig tied to the end of the fluorocarbon leader.

Bob Coan is the mastermind behind the customized bobber. The problem with the *Float-and-Fly* technique is that many suspended smallmouth simply swim up from below the jig and mouth it on the way up, thus the bobber does not go under. To offset this, Coan cut his Styrofoam bobbers in half and added weight to the inside-top of the bobber, thus the weight of the jig would keep the bobber upright. With the now top-heavy bobber, when a fish would *"mouth"* the jig and move upward in the water table, it would remove the weight on the bobber and the bobber would tip over on its side to indicate a strike. Problem solved! "Bob is the one who came up with putting weight in the top of the bobber to indicate when a fish had taken the jig," says Headrick.

The jig used in the *Float-and-Fly* technique is also a specialty item. Most are poured using a *Do-It* Model JM-7-A minnow head jig mold in 1/16 or 1/32 ounce sizes on a #2 *Mustad* 32756, or *Eagle Claw* 570 or 575 Aberdeen jig hook. Combinations of craft hair or duck feathers are tied onto the jig to simulate small bait fish which Dale Hollow smallmouth feed on in the winter. I prefer to paint my jig heads white and highlight the raised eyes with a yellow background and black pupil. Most jigs that are tied with craft hair use a combination of three colors, for example, a white horizontal center with a blue top and orange or red bottom accent to simulate the gill area. I will also tie some jigs with barred duck feathers instead of craft hair, but will still add the craft hair accent to the gill area. I use *Danville's* 210 Denier tying thread and match the color to the gill accent color. Anglers who don't want to go to all the trouble of casting and tying their own jigs or customizing their own bobbers can purchase these items through *Punisher Lures* in Celina, Tennessee.

    Bluff banks and deep points are an excellent starting place to search for suspended winter smallmouth at Dale Hollow. I have found that when the Army Corp of Engineers is generating that smallmouth tend to position themselves on deep banks on the main lake above the river channel to take advantage of the current and catch a meal that might float by. When the generators are not running bass may still be positioned on the main lake, but also may move onto deep secondary points.

Fishing Southern Kentucky and Northern Tennessee Waters

Successful anglers use their graph to pinpoint the location and depth of either suspended fish or baitfish. Knowing this preferred depth allows the angler to determine the length of the fluorocarbon leader line so that the jig can be dangled at the exact position bass are positioned in the water table.

Presentation is key... remember that it must be S-L-O-W. Even if you think you are fishing slowly, S-L-O-W down even more. The beauty of the craft hair jig is that craft hair does not absorb water and will *"breathe"* with the slightest motion, even the almost undetectable current will cause the hair to pulsate. If the wind is dead calm, the angler can twitch the rod slightly every now and then and then allow it to sit again. When there is a breeze, allow the wind to carry your bobber and the chop on the surface to impart action to your jig.

The longer rod length allows the casting of the long leader line, but the limberness of the rod also takes the brunt of the fight of the fish. Set the drag on your spinning reel so that it keeps some pressure on the line and keeps the rod bent during the fight, but no so tight that a sudden lunge of the fish will break the line.

Prime water temperature for using the *Float-and-Fly* for smallmouth is from 55 down to 50 degrees. "I have caught some of the biggest smallmouth of the season with the water temperature at 55 degrees," says Headrick. Once the temperature drops below 50 degrees the duck feather jigs seem to be better producers than those tied with craft hair.

Dress warm, take along a thermos of hot coffee and perhaps a packet or two of *Hot Hands*, and don't get upset if you land a crappie or two in the process.

John Laker with a nice Dale Hollow Lake winter smallmouth.

Cumberland River Walleye and Sauger

Austin Graves with a nice Cumberland River sauger caught while trolling a #5 *Shad Rap*.

River anglers are always happy to see the temperatures begin dipping as the fall season comes into full swing. On the Cumberland River in southern Kentucky and northern Tennessee this means increased activity in walleye and sauger fishing. Understanding the two species will go a long way to helping you put more of these tasty fish in the live well.

The walleye (*Stizostedion virteum*) and sauger (*Stizostedion canadense*) are native to Kentucky/Tennessee river systems and are of the same family. While these two species have many things in common, there are also some subtle differences. Both fish begin their pre-spawn journey upstream as water temperatures drop, but sauger begin the migration slightly earlier than walleye. Sauger can begin to group upstream below impoundments when the water temperature drops to the low 50s, while walleye generally prefer a water temperature of 45-46 before they begin to stage in pre-spawn positions. Another difference between these two species is where anglers find them in the water table. Walleye are often found suspended in slack water close to current, but sauger hug the bottom and relate more inside the current.

Understanding the habits of these two fish will determine how anglers should approach river fishing. In late fall, anglers should use techniques that target sauger since they will be the first to move upstream. Late fall is a perfect time to troll crankbaits for sauger. I prefer *Rapala #5 Shad Rap* for sauger. When selecting a crankbait it is important to select a lure that will dig all the way to the bottom. Sauger are not apt to chase a bait that runs two or three feet off the bottom. The Cumberland River below Wolf Creek Dam to the Tennessee line is not a deep river therefore I like to target the edges between shallow gravel flats (3-4 feet) adjacent to deep water (8-15 feet). The shallow-running #5 is normally perfect for these areas and will work well upon the flat if the fish are up. When the fish are relating more to the deeper part of these transition edges, switch to a deeper running #7 *Shad Rap.*

Fishing Southern Kentucky and Northern Tennessee Waters

As the water temperature continues to fall in late November and early December, anglers can begin to target walleye. Since walleye like to suspend in deeper water, it is best to use the longer stick bait lures such as the *Rapala Husky Jerk*, although they can also be caught on crankbaits such as *Wally Divers*. I still like to work the transition areas between deep water and shallow flats, but for walleye I will concentrate more toward the deeper water. Regardless of whether you are targeting sauger or walleye, expect the more active fish to be on the upstream side of the shallow/deep transition areas and the neutral fish to be on the downstream edges.

It is important when trolling crankbaits that you make sure your bait is running true. If the bait is running to one side you will not get the depth the bait was designed to run. You can adjust your bait by slightly bending the eye of the bait in the opposite direction that it is running off-center. In other words, if the bait is running to the left, (with the lure facing you) slightly bend the eye to the right. Test the bait close to the boat until it runs true to center. Run crankbaits well behind the boat. I normally like to run my bait 75-100 feet behind the boat and will sometimes use planer boards to get the lure out of the boat path. If you don't use planer boards, troll in a zig-zag pattern to keep the lure running outside the path of the boat.

Select crankbait colors according to the clarity of the water. Use natural colors when the water is clear and switch to florescent colors in heavily stained water. But don't be afraid to break the rules. Sometimes both sauger and walleye will prefer one color over another and may change that preference throughout the day. Experiment to see which color they prefer, and if you are trolling more than one rod from the boat, use different colors to determine what is working best.

Kentucky anglers who fish the Cumberland River from Wolf Creek Dam down to the Tennessee line need to know they are required to have a trout permit to fish this portion of the river, even if they aren't targeting trout. The daily singly or combined limit on walleye and sauger in Kentucky is six fish with a 15 inch minimum size limit on walleye and no size limit on sauger.

Mike Turner with a nice walleye caught while trolling the Cumberland River with a *Rapala #7 Shad Rap* crankbait.

The Art of Trolling

Trolling is a relatively easy and effective way to fish. The process involves selecting a crankbait to match the water depth and species of fish you're after, then trolling it slowly on a long line behind the boat. While anyone with a boat can immediately be successful at trolling, here are some tips that can help increase your success rate.

Designed with a plastic lip at the nose of the lure, when trolled or cranked, crankbaits dig into the water with a side-to-side and downward wiggle; thereby becoming one of the most natural looking artificial lures available on the market today. The plastic lip is a very important component to the crankbait. Lip length determines how deep the crankbait will run (the longer the lip the deeper the lure will dig). The width of the lip, coupled with the length and width of the crankbait itself, determine the tightness of the wiggle; stubby baits with short wide lips produce tight wiggles, while long slim baits with long slim lips produce a much wider wiggle.

A couple of factors figure in when selecting the proper crankbait. First, the lure should be the correct size for the species of fish being targeted. Second, you should select a crankbait that will dig deep enough to occasionally scratch the bottom.

Normally, anglers use from 8- to 12-pound test line for trolling crankbaits for the smaller species of fish, but increase line size for the larger fish such as stripers. The heavier the line the shallower the bait will run. According to some studies, each time line weight is increased two pounds, say from 10- to 12-pound test, lure depth is decreased by one foot.

Color can be the key to success. Crankbaits in either shad (silver and black) or crawfish (orange and black) are hard to beat. But often it will be the specific wiggle and depth the crankbait runs that will account for its effectiveness. The combined pull of the fishing line (upward) and digging into the water by the lip (downward) is what produces the swimming action of the crankbait. Damage to either the line eye or the plastic lip will not allow the bait to run true and straight. In most cases, lures that run to one side (either right or left) are the result of a bent line eye. To correct this, hold the bait facing you (lip pointing toward you) and use a pair of needle-nose pliers to bend the eye slightly in the direction you want to the crankbait run to get it back on track.

Anglers who want to get their lines out of the wake of the boat can use planer boards such as the *Yellow Bird* or *Off Shore* brands. Planer boards have an angled edge on the front which causes them to run either left or right. The distance the planer board will run beside the board is determined by the amount of line that is let out. The rod line is attached to the planer board by a clip which releases the line when a fish hits.

Joel Wilson of Glasgow, Kentucky with a nice brown trout caught while trolling the Cumberland River.

Breaking down the Spring Spawn

Mike Turner of Monroe County, Kentucky shows the size of bass that can be caught during the spring spawning period.

Bass fishing in spring is unlike any other period of the year. This is the time of the year when bass spawn and the attitude of the fish can change in a matter of hours. One day you may limit out and the next you cannot buy a bite. What causes these drastic changes in the behavior of bass?

The spring spawn is generally broken down into three distinct periods: *pre-spawn*, *spawn*, and *post-spawn*. In the pre-spawn period fish are staging for the spawn and migrating from deep water to shallow spawning areas and are actively feeding to store energy for spawning. During the actual spawn – when females lay their eggs and males guard the nest – bass are not concerned with feeding, but rather their reproductive habits. During the post-spawn, bass have completed spawning and once again begin actively feeding. Feeding habits, forage, and feeding locations change throughout each of these periods.

During the pre-spawn period, bass like to key on shad. Since shad are open-water forage, bass are prone hunt in schools. When bass are actively feeding on shad, anglers can use larger shad-imitating lures and will be most successful working open water off the shoreline. Once fish begin spawning, they virtually stop feeding. Any lure presented to spawning fish will be treated as an intruder to be removed from the spawning area rather than a potential meal. After a period of recuperation following the spawn, bass enter the post-spawn period where they again begin to actively feed. However, the post-spawn feed is often dramatically different than the pre-spawn feed.

Post-spawn bass will begin feeding close to the areas where they spawned. Rather than keying on shad in open water, post-spawn bass key on other forage such as smaller minnows, bluegill, and crawfish. Since post-spawn bass do not generally school up and pursue open-water shad, anglers are more likely to find individual fish around ambush locations. These locations will generally be in shallow water near some form of structure such as submerged trees, stumps, or contour drops.

Anglers will have greater success by presenting lures with a smaller profile and working them tight to cover.

Once bass anglers understand the different phases of the spring spawn and how they affect the mood, feeding habits, and forage, they are better equipped to adjust their lures and presentations and catch more bass.

Jared Adams with a nice spring largemouth bass.

Technology and Fishing

The fishing world – as with the rest of the world – has experienced a revolution over the past 50 years as a direct result of technology. One would be hard-pressed today to find a bass boat that is not at least equipped with a basic sonar unit, while many are equipped with state-of-the-art electronics that include the latest in sonar and GPS technology. How did we get to this point?

In the late 1950s, Carl Lowrance and his sons Arlen and Darrell began scuba diving to observe fish and their habits. This research, substantiated by local and federal government studies, found that about 90 percent of the fish congregated in 10 percent of the water on inland lakes. As environmental conditions changed, the fish would move to more favorable areas. Their dives confirmed that most species of fish are affected by underwater structure (such as trees, weeds, rocks, and drop-offs), temperature, current, sunlight and wind. These and other factors also influence the location of food (baitfish, algae and plankton). Together, these factors create conditions that cause frequent relocation of fish populations.

Lowrance and his sons took their study of fishing to the next level late in the 1950s, and after extensive research, development, struggle and simple hard work, a sonar unit was produced that changed the fishing world forever. Out of this simple beginning, a new industry was formed in 1957 with the sale of the first transistorized sport fishing sonar. In 1959, Lowrance introduced *"The Little Green Box,"* which became the most popular sonar instrument in the world. All transistorized, it was the first successful sport fishing sonar unit. More than a million were made until 1984, when it was discontinued due to high production costs.

The *Global Positioning System* (GPS) is a space age navigational system that can pinpoint your position anywhere on the globe and has added another technological dimension to fishing. GPS was conceived in the 1970s, and is controlled by the United States Department of Defense. Although GPS was initially envisioned for military use, the Government realized early on that there would be numerous civilian applications as well. Subsequently, the *Department of Defense* (DOD) created two transmission codes; the *P code* (Precision code) for military use, and the *C/A code* (Civilian Access code) for civilian use.

The highest accuracy levels were to be reserved for the military so as to prevent hostile enemy attacks against the U.S. using our own navigational system. However, once in operation, the civilian GPS receivers using the C/A code proved to be more accurate than the DOD had intended. Consequently, the military developed a system for randomly degrading the accuracy of the signals being transmitted to civilian GPS receivers. This intentional degradation in accuracy is called *Selective Availability* or S/A. Effective May 2, 2000 selective availability (S/A) has been eliminated, thereby increasing the accuracy of GPS units. More recently, *Differential GPS*, or DGPS, and *Wide Area Augmentation System*, or WAAS, have been developed to improve GPS accuracy.

But what do these technological advances mean for fishermen?

The benefits of sonar for fishermen are the ability to determine depth, bottom construction, the presence of structure, bottom contour, and the presence of fish or bait fish. These give anglers a virtual underwater picture of the water they are fishing. GPS has further revolutionize modern angling by allow fishermen to precisely pinpoint productive spots and mark them for future reference. GPS also enables anglers to use lake contour maps to pre-mark potential spots and then navigate to these precise locations once on the water.

While there is a wide range of GPS units to choose from – both handheld units and sonar/GPS combos – I prefer a handheld unit because I can use it if I'm fishing out of my boat or with someone else. My unit is the *Garmin* GPSMAP 76 CSx and the following illustrations are based on this unit, although all GPS units have the same basic operation.

The first feature available to anglers is the marking of *WayPoints*. A *WayPoint* is simply a GPS marker to identify a specific location, and once marked, will record the precise location on the internal GPS map. The *Garmin* unit comes with *MapSource* which is a computer program that allows the transfer of data between the computer and GPS unit. If you purchase *Garmin's U.S. Inland Lakes* contour map program to upload to your GPS you will have a contour map of each lake in the United States. This program allows anglers to view the lake contours the night before fishing to determine potential hot spots and mark them so they can navigate to these specific locations once they are on the water. I also establish a *WayPoint* marker at each location I catch a fish for future reference. *WayPoint* markers can also be used to identify underwater structure such as stumps, brush piles, or contour features you want to mark. The *Garmin* GPSMAP 76CSx has space for 1,000 *WayPoint* markers.

The second GPS feature for anglers is *Tracking*. When Tracking is enabled on the GPS unit, a continuous track line will be drawn on the lake map. This feature not only allows the angler to keep track of navigation, but is also a useful tool when you are fishing an unfamiliar lake. You can go anywhere you want on the lake and not worry about getting lost; you can simply follow the Track on the GPS back to your starting point. The *Garmin* GPSMAP 76CSx has space for 20 tracks.

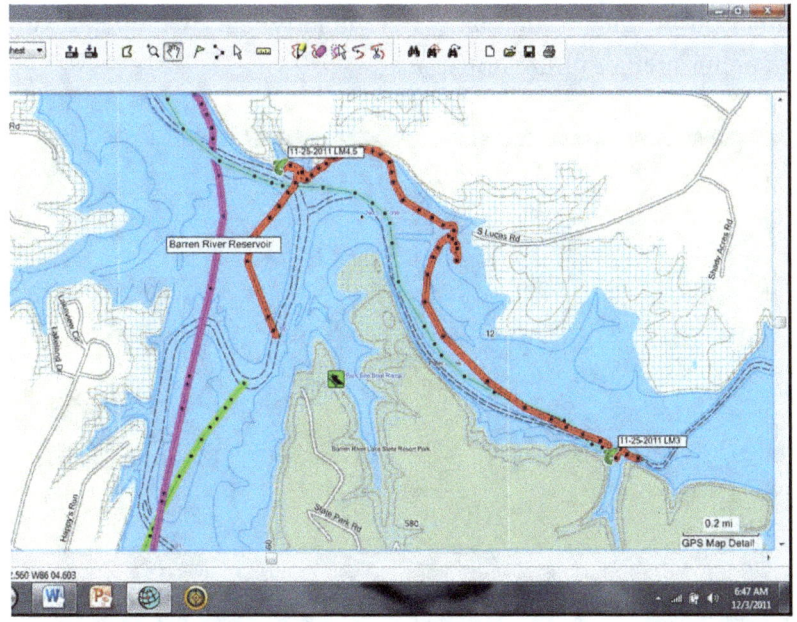

Figure 1 Above is a *MapSource* computer page showing a trip log with *Tracks* and *WayPoint*s (green fish icons) marking catches on Barren River Lake.

When I return home from the lake, I upload all of the day's data from the GPS to computer and save it as a trip log. I will upload *WayPoints* and *Tracks* and thus have a permanent record of where I caught fish, including the precise time and GPS coordinates for future reference. *MapSource* also allows the angler to attach a picture to specific *WayPoints* for additional reference. You'd be surprised how much you will learn about the lake you are fishing by comparing trip logs over a period of time. Patterns begin to emerge that will enable you to better predict future hot spots.

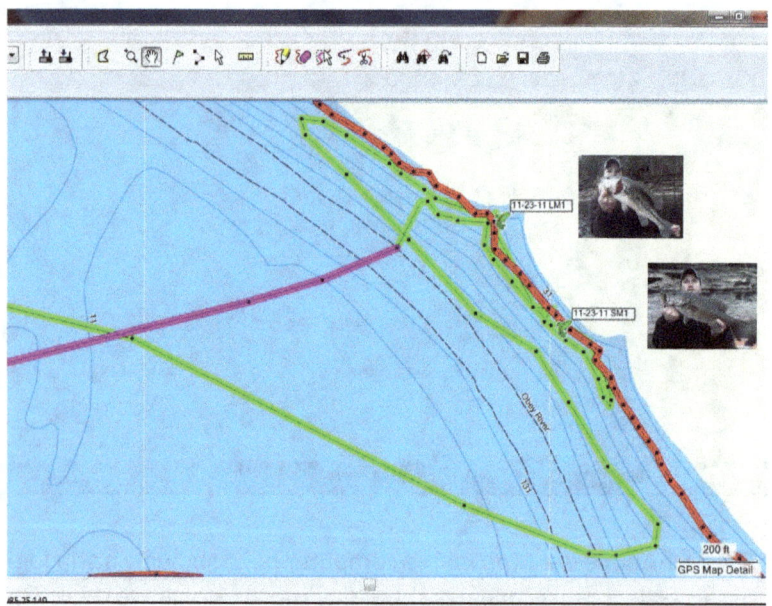

Figure 2 Above is a computer page from *MapSource* which identifies *Tracks*, *WayPoints*, and pictures of fish caught at specific spots on Dale Hollow Lake.

Assuming that Lowrance's research is correct, and 90 percent of the fish occupy only 10 percent of any inland lake, then those anglers who utilize sonar to identify structure and contours that will hold fish and GPS to mark and record those locations will most likely catch 90 percent of the fish.

Fishing Southern Kentucky and Northern Tennessee Waters

Harrell Wilson of Indiana with a nice Dale Hollow smallmouth.

Fly Fishing

My first introduction to fly fishing (if you could truly characterize it as *"fly fishing"*) was in the late 1950s growing up in my hometown of Lubbock, Texas. By chance I stumbled up on an interesting package at the local Army Surplus store which read on the package *"Survival Kit."* It only cost $0.75 so I plunked down a dollar and purchased it. When I go home and opened it up, my *"Survival Kit"* contained a half-dozen flies and a few yards of line with instructions as to how to fish them. I quickly scurried off to Yellowhouse Creek near my house, cut a long slender limb from a tree, tied on a few feet of line and tipped it with one of the flies. I dropped the fly in the water around the base of a submerged tree along the shore and instantly had a hefty bluegill fighting on the business end of my line. I was as hooked as that bluegill on the appeal of *"fly fishing."*

It was many years later that I actually purchased a fly rod and began to tie my own flies. I now have several fly fishing outfits and still love to go after pan fish, crappie, and bass. In the remainder of this column I will share some tips that have proven helpful for me.

One of the first things I had to learn was how to tie the proper knots. I use a short 10-12 inch section of braided line that comes off my fly line. This section of braided line has a loop at the end that allows easy attachment of the smaller mono leader line. I use a nail knot to splice these lines together and found one of the best tools to assist in tying this knot to be the *Tie-Fast Knot Tyer* which is available through *Bass Pro*. The tool comes with complete instructions on tying the *Nail Knot* which is used to splice two lines together and the *Gryp Knot* which is used to tie the fly on the end of the leader. This tool is amazingly simple to use and a must-have item for every fly fisherman.

I also had to learn by trial and error how to cast a fly rod. Like most beginners, I made the mistake of putting all of my force into the forward cast, which does not work with a fly rod. I finally learned that the secret to casting a fly rod is in the back cast. You actually want the force of your cast to be a swift backwards cast, then once the line stretches out completely behind you, simply swing your arm forward in a smooth motion and the fly line will follow. The flexing of the rod under the weight of the fly line, which is referred to as the *loading* and *unloading* of the rod, is where most of the power and control of the cast comes from. Without breaking your wrist on your casting hand, swing the rod up and back swiftly to a 1 o'clock position and let the line stretch out to its full extent, then move the rod forward in a steady motion to a 10 o'clock position. It takes a bit of time to learn, but once you understanding the mechanics of casting a fly rod, you will soon get the hang of it.

 I will also say a bit about matching rods, reels, and fly line. Fly rods are described in terms of rod weight (5 weight, 6 weight, etc.) with the higher the weight the heavier line and reel that is required. Fly line is also labeled by weight to match the rod. I believe one of the best starter setups for the beginning fly fisherman is a 6 or 7 weight outfit. I have used my 6 and 7 weight rigs to catch everything from creek chubs to large creek carp. Many outdoor outlets sell a matching outfit that comes with rod, reel, and line. I like a 7 foot outfit for fishing creeks and a 9 foot outfit when I fish from a boat or have more open space. The shorter rod allows me to fit casts into tighter places, and the longer rod allows for longer casts in open areas.

 One final area that I will cover will be fly selection. There are obviously endless possibilities when it comes to selecting which fly to use and matching the hatch on the particular water you will be fishing is always the best approach. If you do not tie your own flies, however, this can be a problem. I would suggest you purchase an assortment *Adams* or *Light Cah*ill dry flies, an assortment of *Prince Nymph* and *Pheasant Tai*l wet fly patterns, and a few *Woolly Buggers*. I have found these basic flies to be my go-to flies that have consistently produced regardless of what species of fish I am targeting. They have been – if you will – my *"Survival Kit."*

Larry Wilson of Glasgow, Kentucky with a nice Dale Hollow Lake *"Red Ear"* **shellcracker.**

Understanding a Reel's Drag System

Every experienced fisherman knows how much time, work and energy is involved in hooking into a trophy fish. Those same fishermen also know that even after you get that fish on the end of your line, you're only halfway home. The job isn't complete until you get it safely in the boat. But then that's half the fun... working and playing a fish through the fight.

Above all, the angler's most valuable tool in playing fish is the reel's drag system. Acting as a slip-clutch system, the reel's drag allows line to slip instead of breaking under the pressure of a sudden, or heavy pull by an above-average fish. With your drag set too light, you don't have the ability to maintain the needed pressure to keep the fish from *"throwing"* the hook. If your drag is set too tight, surges produced by the fighting fish will cause the line to snap. But with your drag properly set, you have the ability to both control and enjoy the fighting fish all the way to the boat.

Most drag systems work on the principle of two discs that work face-to-face. Constructed of cork – or some or substance that offers resistance when butted against a like substance – one disc is attached to the side of the line spool itself and the facing disc being attached to the reel's cranking and anti-reverse system. In principle, the tighter the two discs are pushed together (through the drag adjustment), the more resistance is created, thereby requiring more pull to cause the line to slip.

The drag system on most baitcasting reels is controlled by a *"star wheel"* located just under the cranking handle. Turning the wheel clockwise increases the drag pressure, turning it counter-clockwise decreases the drag pressure. Drag adjustment on spinning reels is either accomplished through a knob at the rear of the reel, or by a screw directly in front of the spool.

Baitcasting Reel

Experience has taught most anglers the proper drag adjustment for their type of fishing. However, there is a simple procedure that will help those who are less experienced. With your line threaded through the rod eyes (normal fishing setup), tie the loose end of the line to a stationary object about waist-high off the ground (a door knob works fine). Now hold the rod horizontal and point it directly to its tie point. Reel up any stack line. Now jerk the rod directly up and over the top of your head, similar to the way you would execute a normal hookset. A properly adjusted drag will allow the line spool to slip under the sudden pressure instead of breaking the line. Begin the test with the drag set loose, tightening it a little at a time as you repeat the procedure. A perfectly set drag will allow line to slip, but at the same time, will maintain some pressure (at the top of your upswing you want the end of the rod to maintain some bow).

Spinning Reel

Another point to remember is that lighter action and longer rods can be used with a slightly tighter drag because the whip-action of the light rod absorbs a lot of pull by bending more easily than a heavier action rod. That same bending also keeps pressure on the fish.

Above all, once you hook into a trophy-size fish, don't rush things. Settle back and enjoy the battle. Keep enough pressure on the fish to keep it on the line and your drag just loose enough to keep the line from snapping, and eventually, you and your equipment will win the fight.

Fishing Southern Kentucky and Northern Tennessee Waters

Spinnerbaits for Spring Bass

Rain in early spring is both good and bad for bass anglers. It is good because the water flowing into lakes and reservoirs is usually warmer and can quickly raise the temperature of any given body of water several degrees in a very short time. This temperature change prompts fish that have been in deeper, warmer water all winter to migrate into shallower water and makes them easier to catch. Heavy rain in early spring is bad because it discolors the water to the point that fish have a difficult time locating lures. The conditions that accompany early spring are what have made spinnerbaits the go-to lure for savvy bass anglers. Let's look at some of the benefits of using a spinnerbait in spring.

Probably the greatest plus for selecting spinnerbaits in early spring is the detectability of the lure. When the water is clear, bass use sight to target their prey, but when the water become murky, fish are forced to use their built-in radar system to locate a potential meal. Bass accomplish this through the use of their lateral line that runs horizontally along each side. The fish's lateral line is sensitive to even the slightest vibrations in the water and allows the fish to hone in the source of the vibration. Spinnerbaits help anglers in two ways at this time of the year. First, the flash given off by the turning blades of the spinnerbait makes the lure easier to see, and second, the vibrations produced by the blades make it easy for bass to detect the lure even when they can't see it. With its flashing, rotating, vibrating blades, the spinnerbait not only leaves an easy trail for bass to follow in discolored water, it will even spur lethargic bass into aggressive strikes in the process.

When early-spring bass are related to cover such as treetops or stumps, a deadly technique is to cast the spinnerbait past the target and then slowly roll it into the cover. Once the spinnerbait makes contact with the cover, let it bump and fall into the cover and slowly roll the lure over and around as much structure as possible.

This technique has at least three primary bass-enticing ingredients.

First, the bumping of the spinnerbait into the structure is an attention-getter; the more bumping the better.

Second, the fluttering fall simulates injured forage and is especially tempting to those lazy, cover-hugging bass that are reluctant to chase your presentation.

And finally, the change of blade direction created when the bait's fall is stopped and is slowly lifted and rolled upward over the limbs, is often the trigger that will turn *"watching"* bass into *"attacking"* bass.

Andrew Starnes with a nice Dale Hollow smallmouth caught on a spinnerbait.

Spinnerbaits are also effective on bass that have moved up on gravel flats in anticipation of the spawn. Often these flats are void of cover. Fish in these areas will relate to the bottom, and the best approach is to S-L-O-W-L-Y swim the spinnerbait along the contour of the bottom all the way out to where the flat drops into deeper water. A slow retrieve that is just fast enough to keep the bait slightly off the bottom and the blades turning seems to be the most effective technique.

Basically there are three types of spinnerbait blades: the *Colorado*, the *Indiana*, and the *willow leaf*. The Colorado blade is the most rounded and cupped of the three, displaces the most water, produces the most vibration, and can be retrieved slower. The willow leaf blade produces the least vibration, throws the most flash, can be fished the fastest, and best simulates the shape of baitfish. The Indiana blade is teardrop shaped and falls in the middle in regard to flash, vibration, and speed in relation to the other two blades. As far as color selection, generally a gold, florescent red, chartreuse, or copper-colored blade is used in stained water; gold is good on a cloudy day in clear water; and a silver blade is used on sunny days in clear water.

Spring is a time of transition and calls for varying techniques because of rapidly changing water conditions. No lure meets the challenges of this period like the spinnerbait.

Topwater Action

The old-timers have a saying that states: *"When the surface water temperature reaches 70 degrees it's time to tie on your topwater lures."* And it's true. One of the biggest largemouth bass I've witnessed being caught in Kentucky came at this time of the year, and ironically, came when the bass nailed a crankbait sitting still on the surface while the angler was attempting to fix a backlash of line that had resulted from the cast. That's how simple and explosive topwater bass fishing can be in early spring.

Spring is the time of the year when bass can be taken literally anywhere along the shoreline on topwater offerings. But as is the case with the majority of bass-fishing situations, overlooking visible structure during this transition period can be a serious mistake. Stickups, flooded timber, submerged treetops and shallow stumps near areas of feeder water are all worth a cast or two. Aquatic growth such as grass beds and clumps of reeds will also hold fish. Work the edges and pockets for best success, but don't overlook the fact that a grass bed that lies under just a few feet of water creates an excellent horizontal edge. Working these areas with a number of casts can result in pulling a lot of buried bass to the surface. But be warned: not all topwater lures are created equal. Likewise, not all topwater baits will produce with equal success.

Smallmouth bass are exciting to catch, but they are even more of a thrill to catch on topwater. Tony Harlan of Tompkinsville, Kentucky displays a Dale Hollow smallmouth he caught.

Basically, bass seem to fall for four types of surface retrieves. Bass that are in an aggressive mood seem to prefer a fast retrieve that causes a lot of surface disturbance. Buzzbaits are almost a stand-alone lure for this situation. Not only do they cover a lot of water, but they can also tempt some furious strikes. At other times, a slow, steady retrieve will entice the most hits. *Fred Arbogast's Jitterbug* is an excellent choice and seems to be most productive during the still conditions of late afternoon and night. Perhaps the most-used topwater technique is to impart short bursts of erratic action. Literally hundreds of surface-feeding bass have been caught over the years on the *Hubs Chub, Devil's Horse, Tiny Torpedo* and *Nip-I-Diddees* using this technique. The walking-the-dog retrieve of the larger *Hubs Chub* and *Zara Spook* is equally effective – especially for bigger bass. Last, but certainly not least, is the subtle twitch of lures like the *Rapala*. Best success with these minnow-imitation baits comes by casting to specific areas of cover and allowing the lure to sit motionless for extended periods. After 30 to 60 seconds, and even longer in some cases, shake the tip of the rod to make the bait to wiggle slightly. Remember, you don't want the bait to move, but just twitch from side to side. Repeating this process for extended periods of time has produced more than a few trophy-size bass.

Another important point to consider is sound. Generally, topwater lures fall into two groups: quiet ones and loud ones. As a general rule, quiet topwater baits produce better during calm conditions, while the loud baits are more tempting during periods of rougher surface conditions. Experts seem to agree that bass holding in relatively calm-surface conditions are often frightened off by noisy topwater baits, but are attracted to quiet lures offered with a gentle presentation. On the other hand, in a situation with choppy, active surface conditions, noisy baits are easier for bass to locate and will draw more strikes.

Whichever lure and retrieve you choose to employ, always cast past where you expect the strike to occur and work your lure back through the target area. Expect to hook more bass if you wait until you feel the weight of the fish BEFORE setting the hook. Many times bass will slap a topwater lure on the initial hit and then return to mouth it. Premature hook-sets will jerk the lure away before the fish has time to get it in its mouth. For that reason, many seasoned topwater anglers prefer a rod with a lighter, more limber action than normal. The end result is a delayed reaction time on hook-sets, and thereby, greater hook-rate success.

Once you've experienced successful topwater action you'll agree that there's nothing more exciting than those strikes that you not only feel, but also see and hear.

Phil Yeater of Sheridan, Indiana held the original patient for the *Hub's Chub* topwater bait. Phil is shown here with a Dale Hollow smallmouth.

Summer Night Bass Fishing

Southern bass anglers have learned to determine many fishing activities around moon phases. Not only do they have a definite influence upon feeding periods, but at certain times of the year, changes in moon phase can also be used as a time table to remind anglers that a shift in technique is in order. That's the case with the first full moon of June. For southern bass anglers, it signals the beginning of productive night fishing.

Former Cincinnati Reds infielder, Doug Flynn, with a nighttime smallmouth bass caught on a short-arm spinnerbait.

Fishing Southern Kentucky and Northern Tennessee Waters

June is a transition period. The spring spawn is complete, water temperatures are rising rapidly, most lakes are supporting a flurry of early summer boating activities, and as a result of these combined factors, bass anglers are growing less productive with each rising sun.

For the average bass angler, night fishing means some changes in tackle and techniques, further complicated by the inhibiting darkness. That's the negative side. The plus side – and call it a big plus – is productivity. It's amazing how much the personality of a lake can change with just the setting of the sun. But the increased action is no accident; it's the direct result of normal summer influences.

Studies have shown that once the surface temperature of a lake reaches 70 degrees bass will spend about 50 percent of their active feeding period at night. As the surface temperature climbs to 80 degrees, night feeding will increase to about 75 percent. Once the temperature peaks during the summer (90 degrees or above), night activity jumps to near 90 percent. At a normal feeding rate of 10 hours per each 24-hour period, that means bass will be actively feeding somewhere around nine hours each night. With that kind of activity going on after most anglers have already left the lake, it's easy to see that the changes are worth the effort for those who choose darkness over light.

Fishing Southern Kentucky and Northern Tennessee Waters

As far as equipment goes, lights will play one of the most important role in your night-bassing efforts. Most important, you will need a good black light to illuminate your fishing line, but a good white light will also help with chores in the boat and can be used to slightly illuminate the shoreline for more accurate casting if needed. While there are a number of black lights on the market today, for maximum results it's best to choose a model with an 18-inch bulb. These units illuminate an area big enough for two fishermen to fish comfortably and make line like *Stren's* Clear-Blue Florescent glow like a thin neon tube; actually offering greater line-visibility than during daylight hours. Regardless of the brand of fishing line you choose, make certain that it is florescent; that's what causes the light to glow under the black light. One final thought concerning lights: always carry along a flashlight in case of emergencies.

A number of artificial lures have proven themselves as top-notch producers after dark; with selection based on the structure being fished, and in many cases, the phase of the moon. Short-arm spinnerbaits in the 3/8 to 1/2-ounce variety, tipped with plastic or pork trailer, are a personal favorite of mine, and a combination that I find many successful anglers using. The design of the spinnerbait (the L-shaped short arm) allows free turning of the blade on the fall, and the trailer adds buoyancy, bulk, and more life-life action and feel.

Fishing Southern Kentucky and Northern Tennessee Waters

The proper technique for fishing the spinnerbait is to cast the lure out and let it flutter slowly to the bottom; reeling it back to the boat with a slow hop-and-drop type retrieve. Don't lift the bait too far off the bottom and don't lift it too swiftly. Slowly raising the rod tip a few inches at a time, causing only three or four revolutions of the spinner blade, will normally get the job done. Continue this slow hop-and-drop retrieve all the way back to the boat, looking for hits to come on the fall, or just as you lift the bait off the bottom. Be prepared for some furious strikes on this lure... make sure you have a firm grip on the rod at all times.

Plastic worms and jig combinations are equally productive on night bass. The technique for fishing these lures is about the same as fishing the spinnerbait, although these lures can be worked inside heavier cover.

In addition to always wearing a life vest and motoring with care, night anglers should also make sure their boat is equipped with the required lights, watch for rapidly forming fog and carry along some form of insect repellent and plenty of black coffee.

Jared Adams with a nice smallmouth bass caught night fishing.

Targeting Winter Bass

I once heard a very observant angler say, *"If you look at the pictures of the big fish posted on the bulletin board of any bait shop, most of them will have something in common; the fishermen are all dressed for cold weather."* It is a fact that some of the biggest bass of the year will be caught in our area of the country in the period from December through March. This column will discuss some of the top techniques for big bass winter success.

Jeffery Boston of Tompkinsville, Kentucky with a Dale Hollow largemouth bass taken in cold weather.

Football Jig and Trailer

My go-to bait for big winter bass is the football jig and trailer. I have caught more bass 5-pounds and over on this lure than all of the rest of the lures in my tackle box combined. The reason this bait is so deadly on big bass in the winter is that it is the perfect lure to match the location and preference of winter bass. While it is true that many bass suspend around baitfish schools in the winter, it is also true that many big bass opt not to spend their energy chasing the schools and simply hug deep structure and wait for an opportune meal. Dr. Robert Thacker of Michigan did an extensive study of bass feeding habits and found that big winter bass have a preference for crawfish; and this is especially so for smallmouth. Crawfish are not only a source of higher proteins than shad, but they are easier for bass to catch, thus spending less energy. The football jig and trailer is an excellent crawfish imitation lure. But with so many color combinations available in jig, skirts, and trailers, what selections are best?

The color variation of crawfish is a highly debated subject. One of the most discussed topics is: Do crawfish change color according to the moon phase? The question does not have a simple yes or no answer. Crawfish are a *crustacean*, which means they have an outer shell which must be shed periodically to accommodate growth. This shedding of the outer shell is called *molting*. During the molting process, the color of the crawfish can change dramatically. According to a study by the *Southern Regional Aquaculture Center* (SRAC), part of the reason for the color change is that just prior to molting, crawfish absorb most of the calcium from their old shell and store it in gastroliths located in the head and on each side of the stomach for use in the hardening process of the new shell. In a study by the University of Michigan, Dr. B. A. Hazlett also found that certain crustaceans can exist in two color patterns or morphs, alternating between two different color patterns with each molt process. Texas fishery biologist, Ralph Manns, reports that invertebrates seem most influenced by lunar forces, thus changes of the moon phase could trigger crawfish molts and thus account for color changes.

According to my personal fishing logs, I have had success using predominantly pumpkin green jigs and skirts during the new moon phase and pumpkin green/pumpkin orange combinations during the full moon period, but I will experiment with different color combinations if I'm not getting the bite. I have successfully used the following color patterns: *D&L Tackle's* Cumberland Craw, Perfect Craw, Pumpkin, and Oops; and *BC Lures'* Rootbeer Pumpkin Green, Tennessee Orange Craw, and Green Pumpkin. My choice of jig size and trailer is a 3/8 ounce jig with a pumpkin green *Zoom Super Chunk Jr.* trailer for presentations down to 25 feet, or a 1/2 ounce jig with a pumpkin green *Zoom Super Chunk* trailer for deeper presentations. Work these on steep banks adjacent to the channels and target structure such as wood, rock piles, points, or channel bends. Rather than the conventional hop-and-drop technique, I work my football jigs like a shaky head in the winter. Cast the jig out and let it fall on a semi-slack line. Once the jig settles you will see the line bow. Leaving a slight amount of slack in the line, shank your rod tip and apply minimal pressure on the jig. This causes the jig to breathe and crawl along the bottom. You seldom feel a pronounced strike by a big bass in the winter using this technique. Sometimes you will feel a slight *"tick"* or just resistance. Set the hook on anything that feels different.

Spoons and Blade Baits

Bass in clear, deep lakes like Dale Hollow can be found in extreme depths in the winter (30-50 feet). Catching these bass requires getting a lure in the strike zone quickly and keeping it there until you can entice a hit. Nothing beats a spoon or blade bait for deep presentations for winter bass.

Typically, bass in this type of seasonal environment suspend around baitfish schools in deep water. The key to catching them is to locate the baitfish. Cruise likely locations such as bluffs, points, channels, and deep tributaries and watch your sonar for schools of baitfish.

If these schools are deep in open water, about the only available options is vertical jigging. Position your boat over the school and lower the spoon or blade bait to the proper depth. Once the lure in at the proper depth, sweep the rod upward and then let the lure flutter back down on a semi-slack line. Most of the strikes will come as the lure is falling and these hits can be hard to recognize. You might feel a slight *"tick"* or you may see your line jump or go slack.

If you locate baitfish schools adjacent to a vertical or tapered edge such as a ledge, bluff, or point, make a long cast to the shallow part of the structure and work the lure back to deep water. Always let the spoon or blade bait sink on a semi-slack line, then once it settles on the bottom, let it sit for a few seconds (some smallmouth will pick up a spoon or blade off the bottom) and then sweep it upward and allow it to sink to the next depth range. Do this all the way back to the boat. Once the lure is directly under the boat, vertical jig it off the bottom a few times before reeling in to trigger a strike from any bass that might have followed the lure.

If you see bass or shad breaking the surface in open water, cast the spoon or blade bait past the target and reel back to where you saw the action, and then allow the lure to flutter down through the middle of the school of baitfish on a semi-slack line. Often the larger bass are positioned below the schools waiting for an injured baitfish to fall. When targeting bass that are near the surface, I clip my line into the front hole of the blade bait which produces better action on a horizontal retrieve. If I am making more vertical presentations to target deep bass I will clip the line to the center hole of the blade bait.

I often find baitfish schools in the deep tributaries or along bluffs, ledges, or points on the main lake.

Bass Pro offers excellent spoons such as the *Strata Spoon* and the *Deep Creeper*, as well as a variety of different colors of hologram blade baits in the *XPS Lazer Blade*. I prefer the 1/2 ounce lures for shallow presentations (25 feet and shallower) and 5/8 or 3/4 ounce sizes for presentations deeper than 25 feet.

Soft Stick Baits

Once the water temperature drops to 40 degrees and lower, lakes undergo what is called a *"shad kill"* where shad go into shock and twitch erratically as they slowly sink to the bottom and die. This often triggers a major bass feed, especially smallmouth. A perfect lure to imitate the shad kill is any short (I prefer 4-5 inch) soft plastic stick bait (worm, Fluke, etc.) in white or pearl. There are a variety of choices when it comes to lure selections. I recommend the *Zoom Fluke* or *Finesse Worm*, and the *Yum Dinger*; all in colors that imitate a shad.

The proper presentation of this lure is the *"do-nothing"* technique; simply cast the lure out and let it slowly drift down. Rigging the stick bait *"wacky-style"* (hooked through the middle of the lure) on a light-weight jig head, or weightless hook, will slow down the fall and produce erratic motion as the lure descends. Once again, the key to this technique is to present it in productive water. Use your electronics to locate schools of baitfish and present your lure in those locations.

Fishing Southern Kentucky and Northern Tennessee Waters

Winter can be a trying time for anglers. Bass are for the most part lethargic and must be coaxed into striking through slow, deliberate presentations. If you hit the water expecting to catch a lot of bass, you most likely will return to the dock disappointed. Fish slow, pay careful attention to each presentation, and chances are good that the few fish you do hook will be dandies.

Jared Adams of Mount Juliet, Tennessee with a nice Dale Hollow smallmouth taken on a jig in December.

A Tribute to Some Fishing Friends

The people that one fishes with through the years build relationships that last a lifetime. There are anglers in the all our lives that we look back at and realize how big a part they played in the skill and experience we were able to acquire in our sport. Sure, we learn a lot about fishing from our own personal experience, but we learn so much more by fishing with others. I would like to take time to pay tribute to some of the friends who have helped me become a better fisherman.

Ronnie Hammer

Fishing Southern Kentucky and Northern Tennessee Waters

I first want to pay tribute to my late brother-in-law, Ronnie Hammer, who passed away a few years back after losing his battle to cancer. Ronnie introduced me to smallmouth fishing on Dale Hollow Lake when I first moved into the area in the 1970s. Ronnie was also responsible for introducing me to Billy Westmoreland, the legendary Dale Hollow smallmouth fisherman. He and Ronnie not only fished together, but also enjoyed bird hunting together. I worked as an outdoor editor and took off each Monday. Ronnie and I shared the boat on most of those Mondays fishing Dale Hollow, Cordell Hull, Cumberland River, and Barren River Lake.

Lewis Carter

Fishing Southern Kentucky and Northern Tennessee Waters

I also spent a countless number of days fishing with my good friend, and now retired Monroe County, Kentucky School Superintendent, Lewis Carter. Lewis has years of experience on Dale Hollow, Cumberland River, and other bodies of water in southern Kentucky and northern Tennessee. Lewis and I learned to fish many of these locations together, but I drew more knowledge from him than he did from me. I have used dozens of photos of Lewis to illustrate my fishing articles and columns over the years. What can I say... he catches big fish!

Jerry Turner

I also shared the boat with my good friend Jerry Turner for a number of years. Jerry and I fished almost every week of the year either at Dale Hollow, Cumberland River, or Cordell Hull.

Fishing Southern Kentucky and Northern Tennessee Waters

I remember getting to Cordell Hull very early one morning and immediately getting into a jump of white bass. Jerry and I followed and threw Shad Raps into the jump for about 45 minutes and caught more fish than we could count.

I also shared the boat many times with my good friend and fellow guitarist, Jackie Fish. Jackie and I played music together for many years and fished together even longer. Jackie taught me how to catch trout on the Cumberland River and I introduced him to smallmouth fishing at Dale Hollow. We share equal respect for one another and what we learned from our association as anglers.

Jackie Fish

Fishing Southern Kentucky and Northern Tennessee Waters

I worked as Sports/Outdoor Editor for the *Glasgow* (KY) *Daily Times* for a number of years and had the pleasure of sharing the boat with *Times* General Manager, Bill Tinsley. Bill is an avid bass fisherman and taught me much about his home water, Barren River Lake. Bill and I fished together on Barren, Dale Hollow, the Cumberland River, and many other locations in southern Kentucky and northern Tennessee. I thank Bill for giving me the opportunity to work as a journalist, and at the same time, do what I love... fish with the best and write about it.

Bill Tinsley

I owe most of my knowledge to fishing the Cumberland River to veteran river angler, Frank Petett. Frank worked as an educator and coach for the Monroe County, Kentucky school system until his retirement. Frank and I fished numerous waters in Kentucky and Tennessee, but his staple was the Cumberland River.

One of the more memorable trips that we took on the Cumberland River was a day when we were trolling for walleye, sauger, and trout. Frank looked up the river and said, "There is a treetop floating down the river that we need to keep an eye on." I looked, and sure enough, what looked like a tree was about 300 yards upriver floating toward us. As it got closer to us, we were both surprised to see one of the biggest whitetail bucks either of us had ever seen swimming down the river. We each counted 16 points on the massive rack of the deer.

Frank Petett

My brother-in-law, Mike Turner, and I have shared many passions over the years. In addition to fishing, we have also hunted Indian arrowheads together and have spent countless hours metal detecting historical sites. Mike is an excellent fisherman and lure maker. In fact, Mike probably is the best jig fisherman I have ever fished with and makes some of the finest jigs in the country. Mike's jigs are currently being used by a number of professional anglers throughout the country with great success.

Mike Turner

Fishing Southern Kentucky and Northern Tennessee Waters

So there you have it. I cannot really take any credit for what I know about fishing. I owe it all to the men I have shared the boat with and learned from their vast knowledge of the sport.

Now, go fishing and develop some lifelong relationships.

NOTES:

www.ingramcontent.com/pod-product-compliance
Lightning Source LLC
Chambersburg PA
CBHW072104290426
44110CB00014B/1816